Family of Instruments

Joseph S. Renzulli

Routledge
Taylor & Francis Group

NEW YORK AND LONDON

First published in 1997 by Prufrock Press Inc.

Published in 2021 by Routledge
605 Third Avenue, New York, NY 10017
2 Park Square, Milton Park, Abingdon, Oxon OX14 4RN

Routledge is an imprint of the Taylor & Francis Group, an informa business

Copyright © 1997 by Taylor & Francis Group

Layout design: Siamak Vahidi

ISBN: 9780936386690 (pbk)

Table of Contents

My Interest in Interests

Researchers who investigate all aspects of human learning quickly discover that interest is a very important factor in both the efficiency of learning and the degree of excitement and involvement that young people experience as they go about the business of becoming more effective students. Anyone who has ever worked with young people, whether they be professional educators, parents, or other adults guiding the activities of young learners, knows immediately and intuitively about the importance that interest plays in learning. It is for this reason that interest assessment has always been a keystone in the identification and program development models that I have worked on during the past several years.

Interest, like many other common-sense terms with which researchers deal, is a very useful but often elusive concept. It is for this reason that I set out several years ago to try and "get a handle" on this important, but sometimes slippery concept. Interest is a useful concept in everyday communication, but it is frequently a difficult one to define precisely. My early research resulted in an instrument that didn't necessarily define interest, but provided a vehicle for eliciting information about the interests of young people and analyzing this information in a systematic fashion. The first *Interest-A-Lyzer* was based on field tests and exploratory research activities in a number of school districts. Although modifications to this instrument have taken place over the years, the essential structure parallels the broad range of subject areas in which students might develop strong interests and serves as a stepping stone for young people who need to refine and focus broad interest areas into researchable and investigatible questions.

In the years following the development of the original *Interest-A-Lyzer*, a number of related instruments have helped to expand the assessment process across a broader range of age levels and subject areas, especially those relating to the Arts.

I am indebted to several persons who have participated in this ongoing developmental project and would like to begin by acknowledging the authors of the various instrument assessment techniques that are described in this manual. Ann McGreevy developed the first *Interest-A-Lyzer* for young students. This instrument, entitled *My Book of Things and Stuff*, allows teachers and parents to explore a variety of activities that tap into interest areas with primary age students.

Thomas Hébert and Michele Femc-Sorensen joined me in the challenging task of extending interest assessment concepts to populations of secondary students. The *Secondary Interest-A-Lyzer* allows middle and high school students to investigate interest areas within the context of real-life questions and problems.

Two *Interest-A-Lyzers* that focus specifically on the Arts were developed by Vidabeth Bensen. The parallel forms of the *Art Interest-A-Lyzers* examine domain specific interest areas for students at various age and grade levels.

Mary Rizza developed and carried out research studies based on the *Primary Interest-A-Lyzer* and served as a major editor and organizer of this manual. Her organizational skills and understanding of the instruments across age and subject areas has been especially valuable in the production of this publication.

Del Siegle contributed excellent design concepts to the various instruments and Siamak Vahidi was responsible for the layout and formatting of this manual and all its related family of instruments.

Karen Kettle reformatted the original *Interest-A-Lyzer* and helped to ensure a parallel format for the various instruments.

Family of Instruments

Introduction

The purpose of this manual is to introduce the reader to procedures for using a series of instruments that are designed to assess various aspects of student interests. The *Interest-A-Lyzer* "Family of Instruments" consists of six separate instruments, each targeted toward particular age groups and, in two cases, domain specific interest in the Arts. The six instruments are:

The *Interest-A-Lyzer* (Elementary to Middle School)
The *Primary Interest-A-Lyzer* (Primary/Early Elementary School)
The *Secondary Interest-A-Lyzer* (Middle to High School)
The *Primary Art Interest-A-Lyzer* (Early Elementary School)
The *Art Interest-A-Lyzer* (Elementary through High School)
My Book of Things and Stuff (Primary/Elementary School)

A brief description of each instrument is presented in a later section of this manual and sample pages from the instruments are included in Appendix A.

These instruments can be used independently or as part of a comprehensive model for talent development in all students. A description of this comprehensive plan for talent development can be found in the following two books published by Creative Learning Press:

The Schoolwide Enrichment Model:
A Comprehensive Plan for Educational Excellence
by Joseph S. Renzulli and Sally M. Reis.

Schools for Talent Development:
A Practical Plan for Total School Improvement
by Joseph S. Renzulli.

A major component of the Talent Development model, upon which our interest assessment focuses, is the Total Talent Portfolio (TTP). The TTP is a vehicle for systematically gathering, recording, and using information about student strengths and potential strengths in three categories--abilities, interests, and learning style preferences. Best-case samples of students' work, as well as information resulting from interest and learning style assessment scales, are reviewed and analyzed cooperatively by students and teachers in order to make meaningful decisions about necessary curricular modifications and enrichment opportunities that capitalize on students' strengths and interests. For more information about the Total Talent Portfolio, please refer to:

The Total Talent Portfolio: A Manual for Teachers
by Jeanne H. Purcell and Joseph S. Renzulli.
Published by Creative Learning Press.

The Role of Interests in Human Performance

All cognitive behavior is enhanced as a function of the degree of interest that is present in an act of learning, wherever that cognitive behavior may be on the continuum from basic skill learning to higher levels of creative productivity. The relationship between interest and learning was undoubtedly recognized by the first humans on earth, and it became a topic of scientific inquiry in the 19th century when philosophers recognized the close relationship between interest and learning (Herbart, 1806/1965, 1841/1965; James, 1890). Dewey (1913) and Thorndike (1935) called attention to the important role that interests played in all forms and levels of learning. They also recognized the importance of the interestingness of tasks and objects[1] as well as the personal characteristics of the learner. Piaget (1981) argued that all intellectual functioning depends on the energizing role that is played by affective processes such as interests, and he used the term *energetic* to describe this dimension of human information processing.

Numerous empirical studies have also demonstrated that individual interests have profound influences on learning (Krapp, 1989; Renninger, 1989; Schiefele, 1988), and developmental theorists have acknowledged the importance of interests. Albert and Runco (1986) state that it is primarily in those areas in which one takes a deep personal interest and has staked a salient aspect of one's identity that the more individualized and creative components of one's personality are energized (p. 343). Gruber (1986) argued that the main force in the self-construction of the extraordinary is the person's own activities and interests. Gruber also maintained that the shaping of a creative life may not necessarily involve precocity, early achievement, and single-mindedness, qualities that many scholars have attributed to high achieving young people.

> A passionate interest in what you do is the secret of enjoying life, perhaps even the secret of a long life; whether it is helping old people or children or making cheese or growing earthworms.
>
> – *Julia Child*

---

[1] The interestingness of a task or object is viewed as a property of the task or object rather than a property of the person. Interestingness does, however, have the power to promote personal interests in the learner.

> ...the single best indicator of college majors and expressions of career choice on the part of young adults has been intensive involvement in self-selected projects based on early interests.

Research studies that have examined the long range effects of participation in programs based on the Enrichment Triad Model (Renzulli, 1977b) have indicated that the single best indicator of college majors and expressions of career choice on the part of young adults has been intensive involvement in self-selected projects based on early interests (Hébert, 1993). We also have learned that high achieving students who participated in enrichment programs for 5 years or longer and displayed higher levels of creative productivity than their equally able peers were remarkably similar to their peers, with one notable exception. The more creatively productive group displayed early, consistent, and more intense interests (Reis, 1981).

Although this research does not unravel the mystery of why interests are formed, the procedures used in enrichment programs may provide some clues about how educators can promote interest development. First, general interest assessment information is gathered through an informal instrument called the *Interest-A-Lyzer* (Renzulli, 1977a) or a parallel form of the instrument specifically designed for primary age students entitled *My Book of Things and Stuff* (McGreevy, 1982). Next, a variety of interest development activities based on the general categories of interests for a given group are provided. An effort is made to select activities (e.g., speakers, demonstrations, visitations, etc.) within any given category that are likely to promote excitement and motivation. Subsequent discussions and debriefings are designed to explore potential follow-up investigations, but the follow-up must adhere to guidelines based on the *modus operandi* of the practicing professional rather than the lesson learner (Renzulli, 1977b). Student choice is the key ingredient in determining whether or not follow-up should be pursued. At this point, every effort must be made to promote interestingness of tasks or objects at each progressively complex level of involvement with the topic.

Interestingness of tasks and task commitment are interdependent constructs. One of the most frequently asked questions about both young people and adults who have expressed intense interest in a particular topic is: Where does task commitment come from? Although the answer to this question is undoubtedly a complex one, a major contribution to what may be called the energizing function is unquestionably the interaction between the amount of energy that is part of the individual's personality and physical make-up on one hand, and the interestingness of the task or object on the other.

Not all tasks and objects within a given domain are created equal so far as interestingness is concerned, and unfortunately there has been very little research that deals directly with ways of evaluating interestingness. Amabile (1989) reviewed several studies dealing with the ways in which work environments influenced creativity and Ward (1969) found that children who pursued creativity tasks in an environmentally rich room showed higher levels of ideational fluency than children who performed in a bare room. Feldhusen, Hobson, and Treffinger (1975) found that subjects engaged in a divergent thinking task produced more original responses when provided with verbal stimuli associated with remote responses. If we are to capitalize on what we know about the crucial roles played by interest and task commitment in high levels of performance and creative productivity, it is necessary to translate what we know into practical means for assessing and developing interests in young people.

General Considerations in Interest Assessment

Building educational experiences around student interests is undoubtedly one of the most powerful ways to improve student engagement and performance. In numerous evaluation studies when students were asked what they liked best about their school experiences, the first response almost always dealt with greater freedom for selecting topics of study. Conversely, when asked about their greatest objection to regular curricular experiences, students' comments frequently referred to the limited opportunities to pursue topics of their own choosing. Indeed, many students' views of the regular curriculum, so far as freedom of choice is concerned, are extremely negative. As one youngster so ably put it, "They tell us what book we have to use, what page, paragraph, and problem we should be on, and how long we should spend on that problem." Although enrichment experiences are generally characterized by less rigidity than this statement implies, there is nevertheless much evidence of similar types of teacher-imposed structure in activities that are supplementary to regular curricular experiences.

While many enrichment activities do in fact require whole class teaching and similar types of involvement on the parts of students, teachers must raise some serious questions about freedom-of-choice when every youngster in a given group is preparing a ritualized report on houses of the future, life in a tropical rain forest, or the rocks and minerals of Colorado. This is not to say that every enrichment experience should be "wide open." The teacher's own strengths and interests may lead him or her to place certain restrictions on general areas of study (e.g., futuristics, rain forests, geology), but *within* these broad areas a great deal of freedom should be allowed in the selection of specific topics or problems. In other words, there is nothing wrong with focusing on a general theme such as futuristics, but there are numerous topics, issues, and methodologies within futuristics

> **In numerous evaluation studies when students were asked what they liked best about their school experiences, the first response almost always dealt with greater freedom for selecting topics of study.**

that should be explored by individuals or small groups. If every child is designing a house of the future, teachers may be guilty of the same type of predetermining and prescribing that is often found in the regular curriculum.

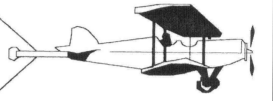

...do not "push" a student into an area of study or other educational activity at the first sign of an interest...

A second consideration in assessing student interests is related to the intensity of an interest and "the way" in which a student is interested in a particular topic. One of the major responsibilities of teachers in interest identification is to make certain that they do not "push" a student into an area of study or other educational activity at the first sign of an interest in a certain topic. Regardless of how much enthusiasm a youngster displays about a particular interest, the possibility of following up such initial interest with more intensive study should be handled with great delicacy. Students should be encouraged to explore different ways to investigate an area of interest and find out the amount of time, materials, and resources needed for such an investigation. It is also important to investigate whether or not the early expression of interest is more than a superficial or romanticized notion about what actual in-depth involvement with a particular problem area is all about.

For example, two youngsters became interested in genealogy as a result of watching a videotape based on the book, *Roots*. The video was an assigned "exploratory experience" that was part of their general social studies program, and both youngsters were aware that if the video was particularly interesting to them, they would be provided with an opportunity and assistance in doing some type of follow-up study. Working together, both youngsters began to look through some books on genealogy. One of these books was *How To Trace Your Family Tree* (American Genealogical Research Institute, 1975). This magnificent little book described in great detail the methodological procedures followed by genealogists in carrying out investigations. It provided several types of how-to-do-it information such as how to construct individual and family worksheets, the names and addresses of all offices in the

United States where birth and death records were stored, the types of inquiries that should be addressed to such offices, and the types of questions that should be asked of relatives in order to obtain accurate information about ancestors. The book also included a glossary of terms used in wills and birth and death records and the types of information that were available from the various U.S. censuses that have been conducted over the years.

One of the things that became readily apparent from these follow-up explorations was that a great deal of time-consuming and very laborious work was involved in such an investigation. This type of detective work actually served to sharpen the interest and increase the enthusiasm of one student, who began immediately to organize and develop a plan of attack. The other student, however, seemed to "drag her feet" in getting started on a genealogical investigation. Further discussion revealed that this student was more interested in the literary aspects of *Roots* and in the social injustice that was conveyed through the dramatic portrayal of the treatment of slaves in the 1800's. This student obtained a copy of the book *Roots*. She read and reread it several times and was referred to other books dealing with the same topic. She did not, however, express the same enthusiasm toward carrying out a genealogical study.

The lesson to be learned from this example is rather obvious. Although both students expressed a very sincere interest in a similar topic that was presented as an exploratory activity, their interests within the topic area were of a different nature. If both students were forced to engage in genealogical research as a result of their early interests, then what turned out to be an exciting follow-up study for one student could have turned out to be a dreary and enforced exercise for the other student. Perhaps some *alternative* follow-up activities could have been explored with the second student such as writing a story or play about the lives of slaves in early America; preparing a presentation about some local points of interest (such as stops on the underground railroad, slaves' quarters or early schools for black children); or perhaps interviewing the descendants of slaves to discover their reaction to Roots, their degree of familiarity with their own backgrounds, or their feelings and attitudes toward this particular time in our nation's history.

The role of the teacher in following up student interest is especially crucial. He/she must not only be able to spot areas of sincere or unusual interest, but he/she must also help the child explore the various ways that  such an interest might be developed or expressed in a creative and productive manner. In other words, teachers must assist students in identifying how they want to pursue an interest, as well as the topics in which they may be interested. Merely being interested in rock music, mystery stories or U.S. history does not necessarily mean that the child will automatically want to become a musician, writer or historian. Such interests do, of course, represent *possible* points-of-entry into the more obvious modes of creative expression associated with these particular fields (i.e., musician, writer, historian) and therefore these modes should be explored.

It is also important, however, to explore several of the other creative modes of expression possible within a given topic or area. To elaborate upon the above example, a child (with or without musical ability) who is interested in rock music might explore this interest further by being a radio announcer or the producer of a rock concert; a youngster interested in mysteries may enjoy telling about them in the book review section of the school newspaper or on a school radio program; and an interest in U.S. history might be manifested in a novel, play, travel brochure, or photographic essay.

The ways in which students' interests might be explored have been neatly classified by Sandra Kaplan[2] into the following four categories:

> *The student may simply <u>store</u> information about the interest for future use or consideration.*

> *The student may <u>study</u> about the interest (as a consumer) by accumulating more information. Such study might be for purposes of enjoyment, personal satisfaction or improved school or job performance.*

> *The student might <u>fantasize</u> about the interest (i.e., child who dreams about being a great actress or scientist).*

> *The student might <u>actively use</u> the interest to generate a project or creative/ productive activity.*

[2] Personal communication with Sandra N. Kaplan, Tehran, Iran, July 1976.

The last manifestation of student interest holds the greatest promise for launching advanced level enrichment activities, although sometimes the third category (fantasy) might also be channeled into creative/productive experiences. The first two categories are important and useful manifestations of interests. However, they are more latent and receptive than active. Care must be taken not to "push" students into investigative activity if their interests are essentially only latent or receptive. These types of interests may eventually result in more active modes of expression and teachers should encourage students to explore them further. At the same time, teachers should respect the students' right to have interests that are not productivity-oriented and avoid trying to channel every interest into a planned follow-up activity.

Overview & Definitions

The *Interest-A-Lyzer* "Family of Instruments" is based on a strategy for helping students examine their present and potential interests. These instruments are questionnaires that are designed to assist students in exploring their individual areas of interest. There is an *Interest-A-Lyzer* that can be used with students at every grade level.

The items on the *Interest-A-Lyzers* consist of a variety of real and hypothetical situations to which students are asked to respond in terms of the choices they would make (or have made) if they were involved in similar situations. Each instrument can be used in group situations or with individual students.

We, as teachers, must help youngsters to identify both areas of interest and the ways in which those interests can be expressed in a creative/productive manner.

Whether it is part of one student's Total Talent Portfolio or used for planning enrichment activities for the whole class, the *Interest-A-Lyzer* provides an opportunity for programming that includes the student's ideas. It allows for young people to add their interests into a framework that can offer direction to present and future investigations.

Although each instrument is unique and designed to be used with a target population or interest area, the administration and interpretation has been standardized across all instruments. Therefore, no matter what instrument teachers use, whether it is the general *Interest-A-Lyzer*, *Primary Interest-A-Lyzer*, *Secondary Interest-A-Lyzer*, *My Book of Things and Stuff* or one of the *Art Interest-A-Lyzers*, they can use the same set of instructions for administration.

Included in the *Interest-A-Lyzer* "Family of Instruments" are:

The *Interest-A-Lyzer*: The *Interest-A-Lyzer* represents a planned strategy for helping upper elementary and middle school students examine their present potential interests through a series of open-ended questions. The general areas of interest identified by this instrument are listed in the box on the following page.

> The main purpose of the *Interest-A-Lyzer* is to "open up" communication both within the student and between the student and his/her teacher. It is also designed to facilitate discussion between and among groups of students with similar interests who are attempting to identify areas in which they might like to pursue advanced level studies.

The *Primary Interest-A-Lyzer*: The *Primary Interest-A-Lyzer*, which uses a format similar to the general *Interest-A-Lyzer*, examines the potential interests of students in grades K-3. General interest areas are listed on the following page.

The *Secondary Interest-A-Lyzer*: The *Secondary Interest-A-Lyzer* was designed with high school students in mind. The open-ended questions tap into the more advanced interest pursuits of older students. The interest areas examined by this instrument are similar to those on the

Interest-A-Lyzer and *Primary Interest-A-Lyzer*. The noticable change can be seen in the wording and examples, which are appropriate for students in grades 9-12.

The *Art Interest-A-Lyzer*: New to the *Interest-A-Lyzer* "Family of Instruments," the *Art Interest A-Lyzer* gives students a format to explore a wide variety of interests in the field of art. Designed for elementary and middle school students, the questions on the *Art Interest-A-Lyzer* cluster around the areas commonly pursued by artists from the fields listed below.

GENERAL INTEREST AREAS

1. **Performing Arts**
2. **Creative Writing &** **Journalism**
3. **Mathematics**
4. **Business Management**
5. **Athletics**
6. **History**
7. **Social Action**
8. **Fine Arts and Crafts**
9. **Science**
10. **Technology**

The *Primary* Art *Interest-A-Lyzer*: Based on the premise that artistic talent is not age-specific, the Primary Art *Interest-A-Lyzer* offers young students a medium for exploring present and potential interest in a variety of artistic mediums. The interest areas are similar to those on the Art *Interest-A-Lyzer*, but they are geared towards a younger audience.

ART INTEREST AREAS

1. Painting
2. Drawing
3. Photography
4. Sculpture
5. Printmaking
6. Commercial Art
7. Art History

My Book of Things and Stuff: Specifically designed to assess interests in young children, this interest questionnaire is comprised of 40 illustrated items that tap into general interest areas and learning styles of youngsters. This instrument encourages one-on-one interaction with children and offers an ideal way to involve parents in the planning process.

Administration & Interpretation

One of the best ways to help guarantee successful use of any one of the *Interest-A-Lyzer* instruments is to explain its function and purpose to students. Each instrument's function should be explained as an opportunity to allow youngsters to explore a broad range of present and potential interests so that they can make meaningful decisions about activities and areas of study they might like to pursue. Although pursuing activities based on students' interests may be only one of several objectives that are part of the overall goals of schooling, it is extremely important for students to know how the *Interest-A-Lyzer* and the objectives dealing with student interests are related.

This relationship can be clarified by discussing objectives related to self-selected learning opportunities and going over the directions outlined on the *Interest-A-Lyzer*. A free and open discussion should lead students to the conclusion that the instrument is indeed an honest attempt to help them explore a wide variety of interests and subsequently "focus in" on a particular topic or problem area.

When working with students on the *Interest-A-Lyzer*, the analogy of an intersecting floodlight and spotlight has been used. It may help to discuss the use of a floodlight to "blast all over the place" without having clear-cut boundaries, while a spotlight is much more concentrated and intense.

Starting with the wider scope (i.e. the floodlight) allows for more interest areas to emerge. In other words, we first want to explore widely and then select and focus from among the broad areas we have explored (i.e. the spotlight). For example, a student could start with an interst in language arts. As he/she explores several types of writing, he/she might zero in on one genre (eg., poetry). The focus may, in turn, spark an interest in a more specialized type of poetry such as limericks or haiku.

Administration

The first consideration when administering the *Interest-A-Lyzer* is time. Successful completion of this type of instrument involves allowing for the incubation of ideas and a full consideration of interests. Teachers should avoid asking students to complete the *Interest-A-Lyzer* "on the spot." It has been found that if immediate responses are called for, many students will give superficial answers. The teacher should suggest that students read the items, think about them for a few days, review the items a second or third time, and finally record their answers.

Teachers should remind students about the assignment each day and ask about the status of their ideas. Teachers can ask students to jot down ideas in their journal or notebook as they come to mind so that the ideas will be readily available when they complete the instrument. Teachers may also invite students to discuss the instrument with their parents. However, it is important to emphasize that it is the students' rather than parents' opinions that are being sought. It is also a good idea to suggest that students do not discuss their thoughts with classmates or friends. Remind students that opportunities for group discussion and sharing will be provided after the *Interest-A-Lyzer* has been completed, and that at this initial stage of the process, the major goal is to find out what kinds of responses they come up with "on their own."

Interpretation

Interpretation of the *Interest-A-Lyzer* "Family of Instruments" can continue to be looked at from a general point of view. There will be differences in interpretation, particularly in the categories of general interest (see page 12). As will be seen, even when looking at specific instruments, such as the Art *Interest-A-Lyzers*, there are general topics that will be explored before narrowing down to specific ideas and projects.

Once any *Interest-A-Lyzer* is completed, analysis of responses involves a two-step process.

STEP ONE: Assessing General Patterns of Interest

The first step proceeds in a way that allows for general patterns to emerge. The major interest area patterns that might become apparent from the instrument include those listed on page 12 of this manual.

Remember that the categories are general fields or families of interests. There are numerous ways in which an individual might be interested in any particular field. Keep in mind that identifying general patterns is only the first step in interest analysis. General interests must be refined and focused so that eventually students will arrive at relatively specific problems within a general field or combination of fields.

STEP TWO: Assessing Specific Interests

The second step is often more difficult than identifying general patterns, because in moving from general to specific, there is a danger that teachers may "steer" students to such an extent that a given problem may be imposed on them rather than independently determined.

Another danger is that students may be interested in studying a topic for enjoyment or personal satisfaction, but may have no interest whatsoever in becoming a creative producer or first-hand inquirer in that given area. This issue is probably at its highest point during problem focusing, and therefore, it is important to proceed cautiously as teachers engage in this process with individuals and small groups of students.

There are specific procedures for problem focusing and basic guidelines for interpreting responses to the *Interest-A-Lyzer*. The first step involves small group discussions in which each student should be asked to share his or her responses to particular items. If certain students are reluctant to participate in this activity, they should be given an opportunity to discuss their responses individually with the teacher, a friend or an adult of their own choosing. During these discussions, an effort should be made to discover patterns that are even more general than the ones listed on the next page. For example, some students will consistently show a preference for activities that are characterized by "extroversion." These might include being an actor or actress, musician, dancer, or organizer of a backyard show. If these same students consistently want to interact with performers or are interested in visiting places such as television studios, ballet performances, or stage plays, then teachers can begin to draw some conclusions about students who like to perform and be "before groups" as opposed to youngsters who prefer to work with words, numbers, or musical notation.

Some Categories of Preferences to Explore:

 Activities that require precision and accuracy (e.g., editing, scientific experiments, conducting an orchestra)

 Preferences for meeting and dealing with people (e.g., teaching, organizing a "clean-up-the-environment" campaign)

 Activities that show a preference for outdoor work (e.g., growing things, camping, studying wildlife)

 Activities that show preferences for helping people (e.g., serving as a volunteer at a day care center or kindergarten classroom, becoming a doctor, dentist, or veterinarian)

 Preferences for activities that involve color, materials, artistic products that have "eye appeal," and any types of design (e.g., costumes, clothing, play sets, landscape, jewelry, metal sculpture)

 Preferences for working with machines, tools, or precision equipment (e.g., photography, building scenery, refinishing furniture)

 Activities that involve creative expression through music, writing, drawing, or movement (e.g., cartooning, playwriting, composing, choreography)

 Preferences for leadership, making money, or "running things" (e.g., play director, business manager, officer in an organization)

 A concern for legal, moral, or philosophical issues (e.g., circulating a petition to start an animal shelter, campaigning for equal participation of girls in sports activities)

Activities that show a preference for working with computational and numerical problems (e.g., using calculators and computers, inventing mathematical games or puzzles, working on "brainteasers")

 Activities that show an interest in communication using on-line computer technology (e.g., corresponding via e-mail, searching on-line databases for information)

There are, obviously, many interrelationships and areas of overlap in the above examples. A great deal of the "art" of good teaching will call for teachers to sort out interests that have the greatest potential for further and hopefully more intensive follow-up.

Implementation

Follow-up to analysis is imperative for proper use of any of the *Interest-A-Lyzers*. Follow-up might consist of having an individual discussion with a student or grouping students together according to similar interest patterns and exploring a wide variety of possible activities that might emerge from such patterns.

In certain cases where group projects or whole class activities are desirable, it is suggested that an area with multi-faceted opportunities for creative expression be selected as a vehicle for follow-up activity. The production of a newspaper, magazine, film, video, theatrical event, or the formation of an environmental study group are examples of vehicles that allow for the manifestation of several types of interest. Depending on the size of the class and the facility, the activities can be accomplished simultaneously in small groups or by individuals, or as class activities. If a student's specific interests are unrealistic it is important to explain why his or her desires cannot be included (i.e. lack of supplies, non-availability of space, etc.).

An additional step in the follow-up process is best described as a "feasibility study." Certain interests may be outside the realm of possibility because of excessive cost, insufficient time or the unavailability of needed resource persons or materials. For example, one youngster expressed a strong desire to travel to the moon! Although the possibility of such a trip was remote, his teacher did capitalize on the interest by suggesting that the student conduct a study of the lives of astronauts and attempt to determine the educational program and career training that should be followed to maximize the possibility of becoming an astronaut. Other interests may involve dangerous situations or sensitive issues (e.g., sky diving, premarital sex) that might present administrative or public relations problems. A feasibility study and discussion about the obstacles and possible consequences of certain areas will help to channel interests within realistic and acceptable parameters of student activity.

At this point, students who have similar areas of interest should be encouraged to form subgroups for the purpose of exploring the possibility of group projects. Brainstorming sessions should focus on possible vehicles that will allow for several types of creative involvement. Although many obvious benefits will result from group interaction, it is important for the teacher to recognize instances where certain youngsters do not share a mutual commitment to a group project. In these cases, it is probably better to allow individual students to work independently or to team up with another student who shares similar concerns. Since many advanced level students are characterized by high degrees of independence and leadership ability, one of the goals of individualized programming should be to provide opportunities for these characteristics to flourish.

The number of leadership roles in any group project is always limited. For this reason, it is important for teachers to judge carefully between the advantages of organizing a few large group projects or several small group and individual endeavors. The main guideline for making these judgments should be the preferences of each student. Open discussion within the group about roles and responsibilities in group projects should be followed by individual counseling with students who appear to be uncertain about participating. In cases where one or more students express reluctance to take part in a group project, they should not be made to feel uncomfortable

An interest in environmental studies sparked one group of fourth graders to start a recycling program in their school. Some students, with the help of the technology teacher, began a newsletter on recycling to help keep the school updated on issues both in school and around the world.

about striking off in their own direction. Indeed, they should be praised and encouraged for their individuality, and the problem focusing process should begin again.

Field tests using the *Interest-A-Lyzer* "Family of Instruments" have shown that they can serve as the basis for lively group discussions or in-depth counseling sessions with individual students. Field tests have also shown that the self-analysis of interests is an ongoing process which should not be rushed, and that certain steps should be taken to avoid peer pressure that may lead to group conformity or stereotyped responses. An attempt has been made to overcome some of these problems by developing a careful set of directions for the instruments. However, it is important for the teacher to allow students maximum freedom of choice in deciding how and with whom they would like to discuss their responses.

Another problem that came to our attention during field tests of the *Interest-A-Lyzer* was that young children often have only limited exposure to certain topics. For example, Item No. 9 on the general *Interest-A-Lyzer* deals with a hypothetical situation in which students are asked to indicate their preferences for working on various feature sections of a newspaper. Since many students involved in the field test were unfamiliar with the diversity of feature sections, a brainstorming activity was planned in which students were asked to identify and cut out many different parts of newspapers. The clippings were displayed in the form of a bulletin board collage, and group discussions were used to call attention to the nature and function of each section. This activity helped students to respond to the questionnaire item in a more meaningful way. It is recommended that persons using this instrument consider each item in relation to the age and maturity of youngsters with whom

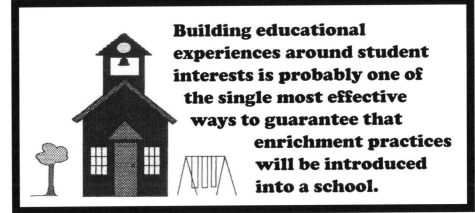

Building educational experiences around student interests is probably one of the single most effective ways to guarantee that enrichment practices will be introduced into a school.

they are working, and that activities such as the one described above be organized whenever there is any doubt as to students' familiarity with the content of the respective items. Teachers may also want to modify or add their own items to the instrument, especially when dealing with very young children or youngsters from culturally diverse populations.

Curriculum planning and implementation either for whole class or small groups can be enhanced using information on student interests. Information and conclusions that result from the analysis of student interests, learning styles, and other strength areas should be noted in the students' Total Talent Portfolios. Strategies like curriculum compacting (Reis, Burns, & Renzulli, 1992) and enrichment clusters (Renzulli, 1994) can be better facilitated once pertinent information, like that found on the *Interest-A-Lyzer* "Family of Instruments," is obtained.

References

Albert, R.S. & Runco, M.A. (1986). The achievement of eminence: A model based on a longitudinal study of gifted boys and their families. In R.J. Sternberg & J.E. Davidson (Eds.), *Conceptions of giftedness* (pp. 332-357). New York: Cambridge University Press.

Amabile, T.M. (1989). *The social psychology of creativity.* New York: Springer-Verlag.

American Genealogical Research Institute (1975). *How to trace your family tree: A complete and easy-to-understand guide for the beginner.* Garden City, NY: Doubleday.

Dewey, J. (1913). *Interest and effort in education.* New York: Houghton Mifflin.

Feldhusen, J.F., Hobson, S.K., & Treffinger, D. (1975). The effects of visual and verbal stimuli on divergent thinking. *Gifted Child Quarterly, 19* (3), 205-209, 263.

Gruber, H.E. (1986). The self-construction of the extraordinary. In R.J. Sternberg & J.E. Davidson (Eds.), *Conceptions of giftedness* (pp 247-263). New York: Cambridge University Press.

Hébert, T.P. (1993). Reflections at graduation: The long term impact of elementary school experiences in creative productivity. *Roeper Review, 16,* 22-28.

Herbart, J.F. (1806/1965). General theory of pedagogy, derived from the purpose of education. In J.F. Herbart (Ed.), *Writing an education,* Vol. 2 (pp. 9-155). Dusseldorf: Kuepper.

Herbart, J.F. (1841/1965). Outline of education lectures. In J.F. Herbart (Ed.), *Writing an education,* Vol. 1 (pp. 157-300). Dusseldorf: Kuepper.

James, W. (1890). *The principles of psychology.* London: MacMillan.

Krapp, A. (1989). The importance of the concept of interest in education research. *Empirische Paedagogik, 3,* 233-255.

McGreevy, A. (1982). *My book of things and stuff: An interest questionnaire for young children.* Mansfield Center, CT: Creative Learning Press.

Piaget, J. (Ed.). (1981). *Intelligence and affectivity: Their relationship during child development.* (Trans.) Annual Reviews Monograph. Palo Alto, CA: Annual Review.

Reis, S.M. (1981). *An analysis of the productivity of gifted students participating in programs using the Revolving Door Identification model.* Unpublished doctoral dissertation, University of Connecticut, Storrs.

Reis, S.M., Burns, D.E., & Renzulli, J.S. (1992). *Curriculum compacting: The complete guide to modifying the regular curriculum for high ability students.* Mansfield Center, CT: Creative Learning Press.

Renninger, K.A. (1989). Children's play interests, representations and activity. In R. Fibush & J. Hudson (Eds.), *Knowing and remembering in young children* (pp. 127-165). Emory Cognition Series (Vol. 3). Cambridge, MA: Cambridge University Press.

Renzulli, J.S. (1977a). *The Interest-A-Lyzer.* Mansfield Center, CT: Creative Learning Press.

Renzulli, J.S. (1977b). *The Enrichment Triad Model: A guide for developing defensible programs for the gifted.* Mansfield Center, CT: Creative Learning Press.

Renzulli, J.S. (1994). *Schools for talent development: A practical plan for total school improvement.* Mansfield Center, CT: Creative Learning Press.

Schiefele, U. (1988). Motivated conditions of text comprehension. *Zeitschrift Paeodgogik, 34,* 687-708.

Thorndike, E.L. (1935). *Adult interests.* New York: MacMillan.

Ward, V.S. (1961). *Educating the gifted: An axiomatic approach.* Columbus, OH: Merrill.

Sample Instruments

INTEREST-A-LYZER
Student Summary Sheet

Student:_____   Date: _____

Grade:_____ Teacher:_____   Rater:_____

Instructions: After reviewing the student's completed Interest-A-Lyzer, decide the general area to which each individual response belongs. Place tally marks in the left column to indicate each instance of a response in that category. The right-hand column is available for a brief description of each specific interest. For quick reference, place an "X" in the boxes next to areas of particular interest to the student.

☐ **Performing Arts**	
☐ **Creative Writing/Journalism**	
☐ **Mathematics**	
☐ **Business/Management**	
☐ **Athletics**	
☐ **History**	
☐ **Social Action**	
☐ **Fine Arts & Crafts**	
☐ **Science**	
☐ **Technology**	

INTEREST-A-LYZER
Classroom Summary Sheet

Teacher: _____

Grade: _____

Students:

	Performing Arts	Creative Writing/ Journalism	Mathematics	Business Management	Athletics	History	Social Action	Fine Arts & Crafts	Science	Technology	Other

PRIMARY INTEREST-A-LYZER

By
Joseph S. Renzulli
and Mary G. Rizza
University of Connecticut

Name:_____ Age:_____

Teacher:_____ Date:_____

Note to Teachers & Parents:

This *Interest-A-Lyzer* is designed for students in grades K-3. It is intended for whole classroom use but some students, especially those who cannot read, may need some individual attention for proper completion. Picture cues are provided for each question to help keep new readers on task and to facilitate with group administration. It is suggested that an adult consult with students and annotate the responses, particularly when students use inventive spelling. This will facilitate interpretation and ensure proper identification later on.

Interpretation of this instrument is similar to other versions of the *Interest-A-Lyzer* and will look at individual responses within the context of broader categories. The more information obtained from the child, the easier it will be to interpret. Whenever necessary, the student should be asked to provide more information by asking questions like "Why?" or "How long?" or "Is that all?" It is hoped that teachers will view this instrument as an opportunity to interact with their students on a positive and enjoyable activity. We feel it is a great way to get to know your students and their non-academic interests.

Remember that there are no right or wrong answers to this instrument and special attention should be given to ensure that each response is true to the student's own unique interests. There are no time limits for completion. In fact, students should be encouraged to think about their answers before filling out this instrument.

What kinds of books do you like to read?

_____

_____

_____

_____

What is your favorite book?

_____

_____

Do you belong to any clubs or teams?

Tell about them here:

_____

_____

_____

_____

Sample

Imagine that you can travel to any time in history.

Where would you go?

_____

_____

_____

_____

You are a famous author about to write your next book, what will it be about?

_____

_____

Can you think of a title?

_____

Name your three favorite T.V. shows here

_____

_____

_____

Sample

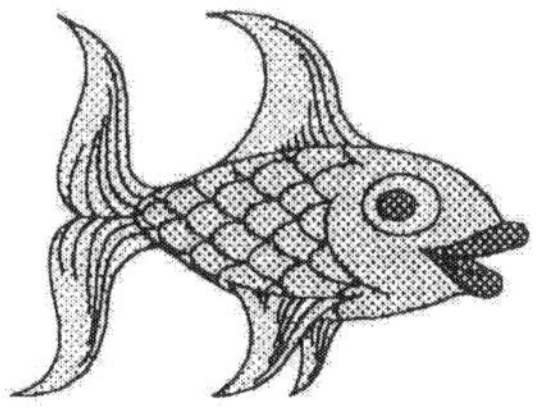

Do you have any pets?
Tell about them here:

_____

_____

If you could have any pet you wanted, what would it be?

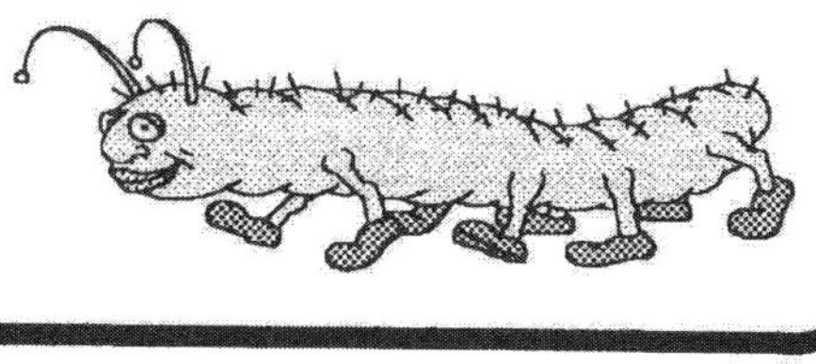

_____

_____

Lots of people play games. What are some of your favorite games?

_____

_____

Have you ever made up a new game? Tell about it here:

_____

_____

_____

Pretend your class is going on a trip and you are in charge of picking the place to go.

Check off 3 ideas from below:

_____ Museum   _____ Science Center

_____ Sports Game   _____ A Show like Ice Capades

_____ Music Concert   _____ Mayor's Office

_____ Newspaper Office   _____ Firehouse

_____ T.V. Studio   _____ Planetarium

_____ Court Room   _____ Police Station

_____ The Zoo   _____ An Amusement Park

_____ A Play

What did we forget? _____

Pretend you are going to move to the moon with your family and friends. What things will you take with you?

_____

_____

_____

_____

Do you like to collect things? _____

What are some things that you collect?

_____

_____

_____

Some people keep journals where they write stories or poems. Do you have a journal?

_____

What are some things you like to write about?

_____

_____

_____

Some people like to do craft projects. They weave pot holders, string beads, or build things with wood. Do you like to do these kinds of projects?

_____

What are some of the things you make?

_____

_____

_____

Some people like to listen to music.

What is your favorite kind of music?

_____

_____

Do you have a favorite singer or band?

_____

_____

Do you play a musical instrument?
Tell about it here:

_____

_____

_____

Sample

Here are things that some people like to do.
Do you like any of them?
Put a check mark next to the ones you like to do.
Circle the ones you would like to try.

_____ go to the opera, ballet, play

_____ make a secret code

_____ help animals

_____ speak another language real or imagined

_____ make cartoons

_____ do science experiments at home

_____ plant a garden

_____ play a musical instrument

_____ sculpt with clay

_____ play chess

_____ build with legos or other blocks

_____ take things apart to see how they work

_____ count things (like leaves on a tree or tiles in the floor)

_____ cook or bake

_____ do jigsaw puzzles

_____ play math games

Do you like to draw?
What do you like to draw?

_____

_____

Here is a blank space to draw a picture.

WAIT! WHAT DID WE FORGET?

DO YOU HAVE A SPECIAL INTEREST THAT
WE DIDN'T ASK ABOUT?

_____

_____

The Interest-A-Lyzer

by
Joseph S. Renzulli
University of Connecticut

Name _____   Age _____

School _____   Grade _____

Date _____

The purpose of this questionnaire is to help you become more familiar with some of your interests and potential interests. The questionnaire is not a test and there are no right or wrong answers. Your answers will be completely confidential. You may want to talk them over with your teacher or other students, but this choice is entirely up to you.

Some of the time that you spend on enrichment activities will be devoted to working on individual or small-group projects. We would like you to work on projects that are of interest to you, so it is necessary for you to do a little thinking to know what some of your interests might be.

A good way for you to get in touch with your interests is to think about some of the things you like to do now and also some of the things you might like to do if the given the opportunity. Some of the questions that follow will be "Imagine if…" questions, but keep in mind that their only purpose is to have you think about the choices you would make in an imaginary situation.

As you read the questions try not to think about the kinds of answers that your friends might write or how they might feel about your answers. Remember, no one will see your answers if you want to keep them confidential.

Do not try to answer the questions now. Read them over and think about them for a few days and then write your answers. Please do not discuss the questionnaire with others at this time. Sometimes we can be influenced by the opinions of others and this influence may prevent you from exploring some of your own interests. Remember, the purpose of The Interest -A-Lyzer is to get YOU to THINK about YOUR OWN INTERESTS.

1. Imagine that your class has decided to create its own Video Production Company. Each person has been asked to sign up for his or her first, second or third choice for one of the jobs listed below. Mark your first choice with a 1, second choice with a 2, and third choice with a 3.

_____ Actor/Actress

_____ Director

_____ Musician

_____ Business Manager   _____ Costume Designer

_____ Computer Effects Specialist   _____ Scenery Designer

_____ Prop Person   _____ Light/Sound Person

_____ Advertising Agent   _____ Camera Operator

_____ Script Writer   _____ Dancer

2. Imagine that you have become a famous author of a well-known book. What is the general subject of your book? Circle One.

Fine Arts   Business   Science

Writing   History   Social Action

Athletics   Mathematics

Performing Arts   Technology

What will it be about?

_____

_____

_____

_____

What would be a good title for your book?

_____

3. Computers and telephone technology allow us to communicate with people all over the world. Imagine that your school has installed an Internet or telephone system that will allow you to communicate with anyone in the world. With whom would you correspond?

First Choice _____

Second Choice _____

Third Choice _____

4. Imagine that a time machine has been invented that will allow famous people from the past to travel through time. If you could invite some of these people to visit your class, who would you invite?

First Choice _____

Second Choice _____

Third Choice _____

5. Are you a collector? Do you collect stamps, coins, autographs, baseball cards, or other things? List the things that you collect and the number of years you have been collecting.

Things I Collect	Number of Years I Have Been Collecting
_____	_____
_____	_____
_____	_____
_____	_____

Imagine you have the time and the money to collect anything you wanted. What would you collect?

_____

_____

6. Imagine you have the opportunity to travel to a new and exciting city. You can select three places to visit. Mark your first, second and third choice by placing a 1, 2, and 3 in the spaces below.

_____	Art Gallery	_____	Science Center
_____	Professional Sport Training Camp	_____	Ballet or Modern Dance
_____	Historical Sites	_____	Musical Concert
_____	Stock Market	_____	State Senate Meeting
_____	Television Studio	_____	Computer Center
_____	Planetarium	_____	Court Room
_____	Telecommunications Center	_____	Zoo
_____	Symphony Orchestra	_____	Stage Play
_____	3-Dimensional Multi-Media Film	_____	Newspaper Office

7. Imagine that you have been assigned to a space station for your next school year. You are allowed to take a few personal possessions (books, games, hobbies, projects) with you to help you spend your free time.
List the things you would take.

_____

_____

_____

_____

_____

8. Imagine that you can spend a week "job shadowing" any person in your community to investigate a career you might like to have in the future. List the occupations of the persons you would select.

First Choice _____

Second Choice _____

Third Choice _____

9.

Newspapers often have special feature columns or sections such as the ones listed below. Imagine you have been given a job as a feature writer. Which of the following columns would you like to write? Mark your first, second, and third choice with a 1, 2, and 3.

_____	Movie Reviews	_____	Fashion Column
_____	Book Reviews	_____	Science Facts
_____	Political Cartoons	_____	Cross Word Puzzles
_____	Local History	_____	Camping
_____	Stock Market Analysis	_____	Music Critic
_____	Personal Advice	_____	Business Trends
_____	Video Game Reviews	_____	Humor
_____	Editorials	_____	Mathematics Puzzles
_____	Famous People	_____	Advice on Chess
_____	Cars and Bikes	_____	Sports Analyst
_____	Travel	_____	Pet Care
_____	Internet Connections	_____	Computer Column
_____	Social Action News	_____	Advice to Consumers

10. Some schools offer extra-curricular activities and clubs that coincide with student interest areas. In fact, students sometimes don't know they have an interest in something until they get to try it out in a club or activity. Enrichment Clusters are another good place to find out about interest areas. Listed below are some examples of clubs, activities, and clusters.

Mark the ones that you have been involved in with an "X". Circle the ones you would like to try someday.

_____ Newspaper	_____ Language Club
_____ Yearbook	_____ Collections Club
_____ 4-H	_____ Ecology Club
_____ Girl or Boy Scouts	_____ Drama
_____ Cooking Club	_____ Invention Convention
_____ Math Club	_____ Science Club
_____ Chess	_____ Literary Magazine
_____ Babysitting Club	_____ Computer Club
_____ Math Olympiad	_____ Future Problem Solving
_____ Odyssey of the Mind	_____ Sports (List here): _____

Are there any we forgot? You can use space below to tell us which clubs, activities, or clusters you have participated in:

11.

Many people take part in activities that are not connected with school work or the extra-curricular activities organized by the school. Listed below are examples of such activities. Indicate how often you have participated in each activity by marking the appropriate column. Please do NOT check any activities that were part of your school work or were organized by the school which you attend.

	Never	Seldom	Sometimes	Often
1. Wrote a short story, play or poem.	____	____	____	____
2. Repaired a broken radio, toy, machine or piece of furniture.	____	____	____	____
3. Conducted a science experiment.	____	____	____	____
4. Programmed a computer.	____	____	____	____
5. Printed a newspaper.	____	____	____	____
6. Took photographs of landscapes, interesting people or unusual objects.	____	____	____	____
7. Studied the weather by keeping daily records of temperature, barometric pressure, rain fall etc.	____	____	____	____
8. Used the Internet to locate information.	____	____	____	____
9. Organized a team or club.	____	____	____	____
10. Organized a musical group.	____	____	____	____
11. Was a member of a musical or theatrical group.	____	____	____	____
12. Put on a puppet show for younger children.	____	____	____	____
13. Started a business (for example: car wash, bicycle repairs, lemonade stand).	____	____	____	____
14. Designed a comic strip.	____	____	____	____
15. Painted or sketched interesting people, objects or landscapes.	____	____	____	____
16. Used a computer graphics program to design original artwork.	____	____	____	____
17. Wrote a letter or sent e-mail to the editor of a newspaper or a public official (Mayor, Congressperson, etc.).	____	____	____	____
18. Learned to play a musical instrument.	____	____	____	____
19. Wrote a song, opera or other musical composition.	____	____	____	____

	Never	Seldom	Sometimes	Often
20. Learned a handicraft such as weaving, wood carving, or making jewelry.	____	____	____	____
21. Designed costumes, clothes or furniture.	____	____	____	____
22. Entered a contest (Example: chess, writing, art, athletic).	____	____	____	____
23. Put on a backyard show (circus, magic show, exhibition).	____	____	____	____
24. Built or designed a vehicle (model aircraft, rocket, hot air balloon, go-cart).	____	____	____	____
25. Developed film and printed photographs.	____	____	____	____
26. Created a spread sheet program to keep track of finances.	____	____	____	____
27. Designed a physical fitness program for yourself.	____	____	____	____
28. Learned another language.	____	____	____	____
29. Made up and used a secret code.	____	____	____	____
30. Used a computer software program to create a newsletter.	____	____	____	____
31. Kept a journal or diary for over a year.	____	____	____	____
32. Made and recorded observations of people or animals on a regular basis.	____	____	____	____
33. Planted and cultivated a garden.	____	____	____	____
34. Started a neighborhood project (paper drive, building a park, recycling program, etc.).	____	____	____	____
35. Read a news, science or literary magazine on a regular basis.	____	____	____	____
36. Raised animals to sell or to enter in a show or contest.	____	____	____	____
37. Made a video.	____	____	____	____
38. Performed as a comic, using original material.	____	____	____	____
39. Designed and maintained a computer bulletin board.	____	____	____	____

The End

Secondary Interest-A-Lyzer

Thomas P. Hébert
The University of Alabama

Michele F. Sorensen
Berlin, Connecticut Public Schools

Joseph S. Renzulli
The University of Connecticut

This is an informal interest inventory that will serve as a foundation for developing your specific areas of interest throughout the school year. The information you provide is completely confidential. As a result of this survey, we hope to provide you with meaningful educational experiences that will further develop your interests, nurture your talents, and challenge your learning potential.

Read each question carefully and provide us with as much detailed information as possible so we may obtain a clear understanding of your interests.

Name _____

Grade _____   Date _____

School _____

1 You are fed up with the course offerings at your high school. Your principal has asked you to design the perfect course for people with your same interests. What would the course be called? What would be taught?

☐

2 Rather than provide money for a class trip, the board of education has decided to give money to each individual student for a trip of his or her choice! Where would you go? List three (3) places you would visit and explain what you would do while visiting there. Why?

☐

3 You have written your first book which you are ready to submit for publication. What is the title? What is the book about?

☐

4 You have been asked to plan a concert for your high school. You have an unlimited budget! List three (3) choices of musical performances that you would schedule for that evening's program.

☐

5

The science teachers at your high school are planning a Speakers' Bureau for their department based on a variety of special topics. Sign up for the **1st, 2nd,** and **3rd choices** of presentations you would be interested in attending from the topics listed below:

_____ toxic waste	_____ nuclear energy issues
_____ health issues for teenagers	_____ greenhouse effect
_____ genetic engineering	_____ environmental issues
_____ endangered species	_____ volcanic erosion
_____ weather mapping	_____ meteorology
_____ forensic medicine	_____ rain forests
_____ robotics	_____ astronomy
_____ entomology	_____ medicine and medical issues
_____ scientific research and methods	_____ ecology
_____ insecticide applications in the environment	_____ Other: _____

6

In connection with a Law Day celebration, a conservative and a liberal attorney in your community have been invited to your high school to debate a topic. What are your three preferred choices for possible debate topics? Why are they important issues?

7

You are a photographer and you have one picture left to take on your roll of film. What will it be of? Why?

8

Teenagers in your community have been asked to prepare individual time capsules for future generations. You are allowed to include 10 personal possessions that are representative of you. What would you include in your capsule?

9

You have the opportunity to work with an editor of your choice on the local newspaper staff. Which department would you work for? Rank order your choices 1 through 3 and feel free to prioritize beyond your third choice.

_____ national events

_____ culinary arts and nutrition

_____ political cartoons

_____ local history

_____ stock market analysis

_____ fashions

_____ personal advice

_____ humor and cartoons

_____ celebrity column

_____ children's page

_____ travel

_____ economics

_____ local events

_____ international events

_____ household management and improvement

_____ legal issues

_____ movie reviews

_____ crossword puzzles

_____ horoscopes

_____ music

_____ consumer reports

_____ business

_____ editorials

_____ math puzzles

_____ book reviews

_____ sports

_____ political commentary

_____ gossip column

_____ **Other:** _____

10 You have had a dream in which you have been transported back in time and have become an active participant in that historical time period. Which period has this dream taken you to? Whom did you meet while you were there?

☐

11 If you could conduct an interview with a man you admire, past or present, who would it be? What three (3) questions would you ask him?

☐

12 If you could conduct an interview with a woman you admire, past or present, who would it be? What three (3) questions would you ask her?

☐

13 If you could be an exchange student in any other country for half a school year, what country would you like to visit as a student? Why?

☐

14 You have the opportunity to learn foreign languages from native speakers. What three foreign languages would you want to learn? Explain your selections.

☐

15 An after school group has been planned to meet and discuss important issues facing young people. Select the 1st, 2nd, and 3rd choices of seminars you would be interested in attending.

_____ contemporary moral issues   _____ peer relationships

_____ national security   _____ world peace

_____ career opportunities & choices   _____ family structure

_____ gender issues   _____ issues in ethnicity

_____ death and dying   **Other:** _____

☐

16 The school board is sponsoring a school-wide Olympiad. Any and all physical-related activities will be featured. If you were to participate, what three (3) events would you like to compete in? Specify if your preference for being judged would be based on individual or group performance.

☐

17 Have you ever designed a computer program? If you have, describe your program. If you could design a computer program, what would it be?

☐

18 A mentorship program is being arranged to allow you to work with a person in the community involved in a profession/occupation you are interested in. List three (3) occupations that you would like to explore in a mentorship.

19 List the titles/authors of your three (3) favorite books. State the type of book (science fiction, poetry, nonfiction, etc.) and briefly explain what it's about.

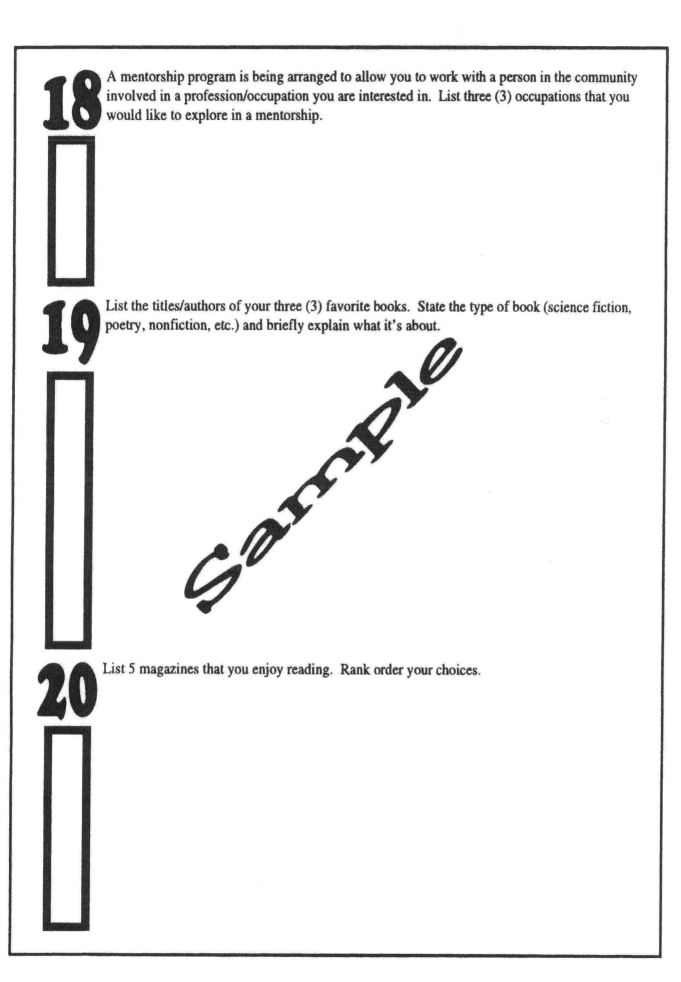

20 List 5 magazines that you enjoy reading. Rank order your choices.

21 Do you collect anything? Briefly describe your collection(s). What would you like to collect if you had the time and money?

22 You have been asked to participate in producing the film of your choice. What type of film will this be? List your favorite three (3) choices.

_____ documentary	_____ science fiction
_____ musical	_____ classic
_____ biography	_____ foreign
_____ travelogue	_____ comedy
_____ fantasy	_____ a popular release for teenage audiences
_____ mystery	_____ adventure
_____ horror	_____ general drama

23 You have been asked to be a member of a social action committee in your town. Your task will be to work with elected officials on issues of importance. What three issues do you think need to be discussed? Why?

Respond to the following questions by checking all of the responses that might apply:

	Yes, I would do this.	No, I would not do this.	I might be interested in doing this.	I have had experience with this activity.

Would you enjoy...

submitting an original writing for publication?	_____	_____	_____	_____
repairing a car, stereo or household appliance?	_____	_____	_____	_____
conducting a scientific experiment?	_____	_____	_____	_____
establishing a school newspaper?	_____	_____	_____	_____
being a photographer for a magazine?	_____	_____	_____	_____
starting an astronomer's nighttime observation group?	_____	_____	_____	_____
studying the stock market?	_____	_____	_____	_____
organizing a new school club or team?	_____	_____	_____	_____
starting a musical group/band?	_____	_____	_____	_____
acting in a theatrical production?	_____	_____	_____	_____
starting a business?	_____	_____	_____	_____
creating a comic strip?	_____	_____	_____	_____
painting or sketching people, objects, and landscapes?	_____	_____	_____	_____

	Yes, I would do this.	No, I would not do this.	I might be interested in doing this.	I have had experience with this activity.
working on a political campaign?	_____	_____	_____	_____
learning a handicraft such as jewelry making, pottery, or silkscreening?	_____	_____	_____	_____
designing costumes, clothing, or furniture?	_____	_____	_____	_____
designing a building?	_____	_____	_____	_____
designing an invention?	_____	_____	_____	_____
having a photo lab and developing photography?	_____	_____	_____	_____
visiting a museum or historical site?	_____	_____	_____	_____
keeping a personal journal or diary?	_____	_____	_____	_____
organic gardening?	_____	_____	_____	_____
being involved in a neighborhood project?	_____	_____	_____	_____
belonging to a social action group like the Sierra Club?	_____	_____	_____	_____
developing and maintaining a computer bulletin board?	_____	_____	_____	_____
voluteering time to a charitable organization?	_____	_____	_____	_____

Sample

Primary Art Interest-A-Lyzer Summary Sheet

Names: _____ Grade: _____

Dates: _____ Teacher: _____

Major Interests:

      Painting: _____

      Drawing: _____

      Photography: _____

      Sculpture: _____

      Printmaking: _____

      Commercial Art: _____

      Art History: _____

Specific Interests:

_____

_____

_____

_____

_____

Primary

Art Interest-A-Lyzer

By Vidabeth Bensen

Name: _____ **Age:** _____ **Grade:** _____

School: _____ **Date:** _____

These questions will help you learn how you feel about art. There are no right or wrong answers.

We want you to work on projects that you like in art. Please take your time answering the questions. Think about them before you put down the answers. Make sure you answer them according to the way you feel, not the way your friends or classmates feel. This is to learn how YOU feel about ART.

1. Check the following things you like to do in your spare time:

_____ Color in coloring books	_____ Look at books or magazines about art
_____ Draw pictures	_____ Go to a museum
_____ Paint pictures	_____ Try different art materials
_____ Others	

_____ _____ _____

_____ _____ _____

2. If you could choose an art project to work on, what would it be?

_____ Paint a picture	_____ Work on a sculpture
_____ Take photographs	_____ Make a silk screen print
_____ Make a collage	_____ Others

_____ _____ _____

3. Which of the following careers in art would you like to know more about?

_____ Art teacher	_____ Illustrator
_____ Painter	_____ Fashion designer
_____ Cartoonist	_____ Fashion illustrator
_____ Greeting card designer	_____ Photographer
_____ Stage set designer	_____ Costume designer
_____ Architect	_____ Museum worker
_____ Art historian	

4. List below some of the subjects you like to draw and paint.

_____ _____ _____

_____ _____ _____

5. What kinds of art work do you like to look at?

_____ Abstract   _____ Realistic

_____ Paintings   _____ Sculpture

_____ Drawings   _____ Prints

_____ Photographs   _____ Others

_____   _____

6. Have you ever taken art lessons or attended art classes outside of school?

_____ Yes   _____ No

If your answer is yes, please tell when and where you took these lessons.

_____

7. Why do you like art? _____

_____

_____

_____

_____

Art Interest-A-Lyzer Summary Sheet

Names: _____ **G**rade: _____

Dates: _____ **T**eacher: _____

Major Interests:

      Painting: _____

      Drawing: _____

      Photography: _____

      Sculpture: _____

      Printmaking: _____

      Commercial Art: _____

      Art History: _____

Specific Interests:

_____

_____

_____

_____

_____

Sample

Directions for The *Art Interest-A-Lyzer*

The *Art Interest-A-Lyzer* can be an invaluable aid for planning lessons in elementary and secondary school art classes and in Talented and Gifted (TAG) Art classes at the either level.

Research and experience indicate that students perform better when they are interested in what they are doing. The *Art Interest-A-Lyzer* is useful for students planning independent projects in art and for class lessons. Without it, teachers may never have known that a football player in their 11th grade art class was keenly interested in interior design. Nor would they discover that a 10th grade girl fascinated by sculpture in public places spent one quarter of the school year designing and making models for sculpture she hoped to have erected on the school campus. Often, students are not aware of these interests until they explore their feelings while answering the questions in the *Art Interest-A-Lyzer*.

Some knowledge of art and art techniques is necessary for students to assess their own interests. Therefore, it would be best to administer the *Interest-A-Lyzer* at the beginning of an advanced course or after a basic course in art has been taken. Some TAG Art classes have been composed of students who had previously been identified as having interest in art. In that situation it could be administered early in the year.

A compilation of the results of the *Interest-A-Lyzer* might team students with similar interests together so they can share ideas and possibly work on a small group project. Discussing the results with students, either individually or in a group, can be very meaningful and is useful to point students in a direction best suited for them.

ADMINISTERING THE *ART INTEREST-A-LYZER*:
The *Art Interest-A-Lyzer* can usually be administered in a class period of one hour or less. Going over the questions first will help students start thinking about their responses. Teachers might want to introduce it toward the end of one meeting and administer it at the following meeting. It should be emphasized that a student's personal opinions are most important, as opposed to those of one's friends or classmates.

SCORING THE *ART INTEREST-A-LYZER*:
The summary sheet suggests areas of specific interests which may become evident from student responses. As you read the completed *Art Interest-A-Lyzer*, add up the responses to the specific categories on the summary sheet. If a student consistently answers questions indicating a preference for drawing, for example, it is safe to assume that drawing is a major interest of that child. You will be able to identify specific interests from students' comments, as well as from the tallies on the summary sheet.

USING THE RESULTS OF THE *ART INTEREST-A-LYZER*:
After the responses to the form have been tallied and conclusions have been made as to student preferences, it is a good idea to have a class discussion enumerating the interests that have surfaced from the answers. Then, groups with similar interests can be formed to discuss possible small group or individual projects that may be presented to the class and the teacher for inclusion in the curriculum. The following chart suggests ways in which the results of the *Art Interest-A-Lyzer* can be incorporated into an art program. Depending on the size of the class and the facility in which you teach, the activities can either be accomplished simultaneously in small groups or by individuals or as class activities. If a student's specific interests are unrealistic, it is important to explain why his or her desires cannot be included (i.e. lack of supplies, non-availability of space, etc.). Whether students proceed to explore their preferences on an individual basis or as part of a small group, the interests of the students will be served. In this way a meaningful and exciting curriculum can be established that will provide satisfying projects for the students and create gratifying results for the teacher.

GENERAL AREA OF INTEREST	SPECIFIC INTEREST	INDIVIDUAL OR SMALL GROUP PROJECTS OR ACTIVITIES
Painting	Murals	Introduce murals and muralists to students.
		Study history of murals.
		Visit sites of local murals if available.
		Visit museums and galleries that may have examples of murals.
		Discuss areas of school or local community which would be available for the painting of a mural.
		Students decide on a mural they would like to print.
		Work up sketches and proposals to include materials, costs of supplies, etc.
		Present same to authorities.
		Proceed with project after gaining approval.
Printmaking	Silk Screen Printing	Introduce subject to students.
		Have students research different types of printmaking and present findings to others in groups.
		Learn techniques of silk screen printing.
		Visit local galleries and/or museums that display prints.
		Visit studio of a local printmaker.
		Research different products that can be created using the silk screen method.
		Students decide on a specific project on which to work.
		Submit sketches to group for decision of final form the project will take.
		Proceed with project.

The above are two examples of the manner in which the results of the *Interest-A-Lyzer* can be used to incorporate students' interests into the art curriculum. Any subject at all can be pursued in this way and as a result, the students will be able to have a say in developing their own curriculum which will be tailored to fit their interests.

ART INTEREST-A-LYZER

By Vidabeth Bensen

Name: _____   Age: _____

School: _____   Grade: _____

                                              Date: _____

Art is a very personal subject. In order for you to become more familiar with the way you feel about art, we would like you to answer the questions in this ART INTEREST-A-LYZER. This is not a test and there are no right or wrong answers.

Some of the time you spend in art will be devoted to small group or individual projects. We want you to work on projects that are of interest to you, but sometimes you have to do some thinking before you know what really interests you.

Take your time when answering this questionnaire. Think about how YOU feel, not how your friends or classmates may feel. Do not discuss the questions with anyone until you have finished it. Your answers will be completely confidential, but if you want to discuss them later with your teacher or classmates, feel free to do so.

The **ART INTEREST-A-LYZER** is for **YOU** to think about **YOUR** interests in **ART**.

1. Check the following things that you like or would like to do in your spare time:

_____ Draw pictures

_____ Paint pictures

_____ Read about famous artists

_____ Read magazines about art

_____ Visit an art museum or gallery

_____ Experiment with different arts and crafts

_____ Work with clay

_____ Watch videos or films about art or crafts

_____ Visit an artist's or sculptor's studio

_____ Others _____

_____

2. Pretend that an art group to which you belong wants to raise money to buy art supplies. Each member has been asked to sign up for his or her first, second, and third choices for a project to work on or make and sell at an art fair. Mark your first, second, and third choices below:

_____ Paint a picture

_____ Make a sculpture

_____ Take photos for publicity

_____ Make a linoleum block print

_____ Make a silk screen print

_____ Make a T-shirt design to print

_____ Make a collage

_____ Make jewelry

_____ Mat and/or frame pictures

_____ Set up the display or exhibit

_____ Make posters to advertise the fair

_____ Others _____

_____

3. Your teacher has assigned the class to read a biography and write a report about a famous artist. List below the artists about whom you might like to read:

_____

_____

_____

4. If you could invite any living artist to teach your art class for one week, who would you invite?

1st choice: _____
2nd choice: _____
3rd choice: _____

5. If you could invite any dead artist to come back and teach your art class for one week, who would you invite?

1st choice: _____
2nd choice: _____
3rd choice: _____

6. List below some of the subjects you like to draw:

_____
_____
_____

7. What kinds of artwork do you prefer to look at?

_____ Abstract   _____ Realistic
_____ Paintings   _____ Drawings
_____ Sculpture   _____ Prints
_____ Photographs   _____ Other _____

8. If you had money to spend on a piece of art to decorate your room, what would you purchase?

_____ Painting   _____ Photograph   _____ Print
_____ Pottery   _____ Sculpture   _____ Mobile
_____ Other _____

If you can, specify which piece of art or artist's work you might choose.

9. You think you might like to become an artist when you grow up. There are many careers in art. Which of the following would you be interested in learning more about?

_____ Art teacher	_____ Museum curator
_____ Graphic artist	_____ Gallery owner
_____ Illustrator	_____ Art critic
_____ Advertising artist	_____ Printmaker
_____ Interior designer	_____ Medical illustrator
_____ Fashion designer	_____ Potter
_____ Fashion illustrator	_____ Industrial designer
_____ Stage designer	_____ Cartoonist
_____ Costume designer	_____ Jewelry designer
_____ Art therapist	_____ Book illustrator
_____ Photographer	_____ Layout artist
_____ Architect	_____ Greeting card designer
_____ Makeup designer	_____ Set designer
_____ Computer artist	_____ Art lecturer
_____ Free lance artist	_____ Exhibit designer
_____ Poster artist	_____ Art historian
_____ Portrait painter	_____ Calligrapher
_____ Craftsperson	_____ Other _____

10. Have you ever done any of the following in your spare time after school or on weekends? Do not include any activities that were sponsored by the school or that were part of your regular school day.

_____ Took private art lessons

_____ Visited a museum or art gallery

_____ Spent time at an arts and crafts shop

_____ Went to an art supply store

_____ Visited an artist in his or her studio

_____ Talked to someone about art

_____ Spent time drawing or painting

_____ Joined an art club or group associated with art

_____ Borrowed art prints from a library

_____ Took a camera along and used it on a trip

_____ Went out photographing (nature, people, local sights)

_____ Sketched while on a trip or while visiting an interesting event or location

_____ Read a book about art or an artist

_____ Read a magazine about art

11. If you were given the opportunity, what would you do to beautify your school building and/or campus?

_____
_____
_____
_____
_____
_____

12. In a short paragraph below, describe why you like art and how you feel about the subject:

_____
_____
_____
_____
_____
_____
_____
_____
_____
_____
_____
_____
_____
_____
_____
_____

MY BOOK OF THINGS AND STUFF

Sample

Name _____
School _____
Grade _____ Age _____

Are you a member of any special group, club or team? Tell about it here.

_____
_____
_____
_____
_____
_____
_____
_____

Do you collect anything like stamps, coins or seashells? Tell about your collection here.

_____
_____
_____
_____
_____
_____
_____

What is the most interesting place you ever visited?

_____

_____

Sometimes we "daydream" about what we will be when we grow up. Draw a picture of what <u>you</u> will be when you are older.

I will be a _____

when I Am Older

Pretend your class is putting on a play. Your teacher will allow you to work in groups. Read all the groups first, then put a 1, 2 and 3 beside your choices.

◯ Work with lights

◯ Be an actor or actress

◯ Work with sound effects

(have a speaking part)

◯ Write the play

(create words and ideas)

◯ Be the director

(get all the groups to work together)

◯ Draw and paint the scenes

◯ Make posters and programs

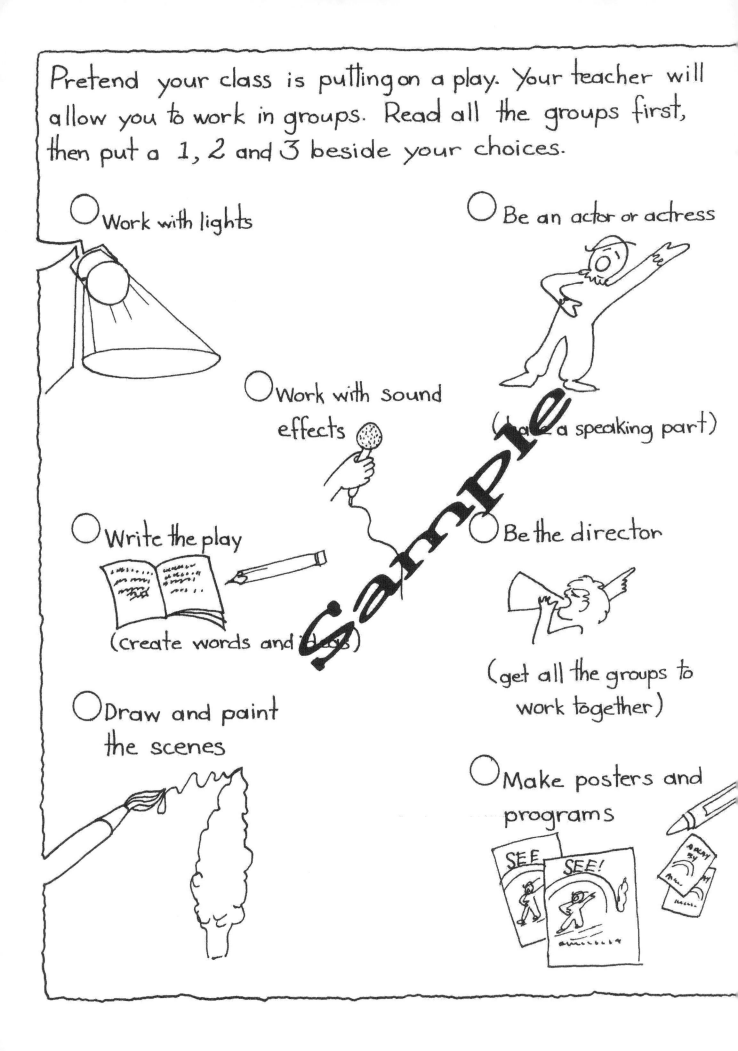

Do you ever speak, read or write another language besides English? [ ]

Français

ESPAÑOL

¿ Habla otra lengua?

Ελληνικά

ΡΎΓΓΚΝΝ   Italiano

Do you ever do science experiments at home? [ ]

Do you ever make up your own cartoons? [ ]

Sample

Have you ever done something you were proud of? [ ]

REPORT CARD

A
B⁺
B
B
A
A

For Product Safety Concerns and Information please contact our EU
representative GPSR@taylorandfrancis.com Taylor & Francis Verlag GmbH,
Kaufingerstraße 24, 80331 München, Germany

Printed and bound by CPI Group (UK) Ltd, Croydon, CR0 4YY
14/04/2025
01844918-0001